Published in the UK by Scholastic Children's Books, 2020
Euston House, 24 Eversholt Street, London, NW1 1DB
A division of Scholastic Limited

London – New York ~ Toronto ~ Sydney ~ Auckland
Mexico City ~ New Delhi ~ Hong Kong

SCHOLASTIC and associated logos are trademarks and/or
registered trademarks of Scholastic Inc.

Text © Omari McQueen, 2020
Photography © Scholastic Children's Books, 2020

Recipe Testing, Prop Styling and Editorial: Nicola Graimes
Omari and Family Photography: Haarala Hamilton Photography
Ingredient Photography: Silvio Bukbardis
Food Photography: Xavier D. Buendi
Senior Designer: Aimee Stewart

Trade hardback edition ISBN 978 0702 30526 9
Schools paperback edition ISBN 978 0702 30642 6

A CIP catalogue record for this book is available from the British Library.

Printed by Mohn Media, Germany

Any website addresses listed in the book are correct at the time of going to print.
However, please be aware that online content is subject to change and websites
can contain or offer content that is unsuitable for children. We advise all children be
supervised when using the internet.

Papers used by Scholastic Children's Books are made from wood
grown in sustainable forests.

1 3 5 7 9 10 8 6 4 2

www.scholastic.co.uk

OMARI McQUEEN'S
BEST BITES
COOK BOOK

SCHOLASTIC

CONTENTS

HI, I'M OMARI McQUEEN!

I'm an everyday boy from south London with a huge passion for vegan cooking.

It all started when I was eight years old and began making vegan dips in my kitchen at home. I started my own business, Dipalicious, and started to sell my dips at fairs and events. Then I opened my first pop-up restaurant in August 2019, and the rest is history!

I've worked with lots of well-known companies and have also cooked on television programmes. I am now a multi-award-winning vegan chef and, guess what? I'm the youngest vegan chef in the UK and one of the youngest restaurateurs in the world. Plus, I have my own TV show!

I wanted to write this book for you and your family, as I love bringing people together through food, without harming animals.

This book is full of fun and delicious vegan recipes with a taste of the Caribbean, as my family are from Jamaica and Antigua. I've learnt how to mix lots of different flavours and ingredients to merge different cultures. My dad was the first person to teach me how to cook when my mum got really ill and could no longer cook safely in the kitchen. At first, it was just helping out getting things he needed – the usual things adults give us kids to do! Then my dad started to allow me to experiment in the kitchen as I really wanted to cook by myself.

So, now it's your turn to experiment in the kitchen, and to cook meals that will blow your parents' minds.

LET'S GET COOKING!

WHAT DOES IT MEAN TO BE VEGAN?

To me, being vegan means that you avoid all animal products for ethical, health or environmental reasons. A vegan does not use, eat or wear any products that are related to animals. Some people think that veganism is a diet, but it's not just that – it's a way of life!

Vegans like myself eat tasty plant-based foods instead of meat, fish, eggs or dairy. But it doesn't end there. This may come as a surprise to you, but vegans don't eat honey (because it comes from bees) and they don't use products like palm oil because deforestation to produce palm oil affects natural habitats.

Vegans do not use any products that have been tested on animals or wear clothing or shoes made from animal products, such as leather or snakeskin. But don't worry, being vegan doesn't mean that you have to walk around with bare feet and no clothes on – there are many vegan alternatives to these materials!

BE MORE VEGAN: OMARI'S TOP TIPS

1. Write down a menu for the week's meals. It helps to make a shopping list with everything you need for the coming week.

2. Get ahead… Some meals can be made in advance and chilled or frozen.

3. Write down your favourite meals and look for their vegan alternatives. There are lots of great vegan egg, dairy and meat replacements available in the shops.

4. Check out the benefits – health, animal and environmental – of the vegan foods available.

5. Read all food labels and double check that the products are vegan.

6. Try different types of fruits and vegetables – even the funny-looking ones! Remember that trying new foods is all part of experimenting with your taste buds.

7. The kitchen is like a science lab and it's fun to experiment with new flavours! Try out different seasonings and spices. Check the label first before buying as some herb and spice mixes, such as all-purpose seasoning, can contain additives or extra salt.

8. I love to use big flavours and hot chilli in my vegan cooking, but if you're new to cooking with herbs, spices and chilli you can start off using smaller amounts and then build up the flavourings.

OMARI'S ESSENTIAL INGREDIENTS

You may never have heard of some of my most-used ingredients before. Here's some more information to help you learn about what they are, and where you can find them!

ACKEE
The national fruit of Jamaica, which is used as a vegetable! Ackee has a creamy texture and mild taste and can be bought in tins in supermarkets and world food markets.

ALL-PURPOSE SEASONING
This is a mixture of herbs, spices and salt. It can include smoked paprika, onion powder, garlic powder, coriander, chilli, celery powder, cayenne pepper and ground cumin. You can buy it in the shop, or even make your own! Always be careful of how much salt you put into your cooking.

BANANA
Look for bananas that are bright yellow in colour – this is a sign they are ripe and taste sweet. Unripe green bananas are also popular in Caribbean cooking in savoury dishes.

BEANS (CHICKPEAS, BUTTER BEANS, KIDNEY BEANS – AND LENTILS)
Beans are great for vegans as they are a good source of protein. They are also used a lot in Caribbean cooking. I like chickpeas, butter beans and kidney beans (and lentils!). Confusingly, red kidney beans are called 'peas' when cooked in the traditional dish, Rice 'n' Peas (see page 82).

CALLALOO

A popular green leafy vegetable in the Caribbean, you can buy it fresh or in tins. I use tinned in this book as it is easy to use – if you can't find it in supermarkets or world food markets, spinach is a great alternative.

COCONUT

Coconut palms have grown in the Caribbean for thousands of years. The sweet, creamy flesh of the fruit is used in sweet and savoury cooking. I use the milk, cream, oil and grated coconut in my recipes.

GINGER

This root is grated and often used as a spice to flavour food. It has a bit of heat to it and can be used in sweet and savoury food.

JACKFRUIT

This is a meat substitute in vegan cooking. Sold fresh and raw in tins, it has quite a mild, fruity flavour that loves spices – jerk jackfruit is the best!

JERK SEASONING & JERK MARINADE

You can make jerk seasoning at home or buy it, too. It is usually a blend of cinnamon, thyme, allspice, nutmeg, black pepper and Scotch bonnet chilli. Jerk marinade is a sauce with a similar great taste that you can use in your cooking. Beware, it can be hot!

HEART OF PALM
This delicious, crunchy vegetable comes from the middle of a type of palm tree. The vegetable is cut into cylinders and looks like a smooth, white stalk. Buy it in tins from supermarkets and whole food markets.

LIME
A squeeze of this bright green citrus fruit is the best on just about everything – sweet or savoury. Like lemons, limes are high in vitamin C.

MANGO
Sweet and juicy, what's not to like about mango! This is just one of my favourite tropical fruits – I'd also add pineapple, passion fruit and papaya to the list, too.

PAPRIKA
This spice is made from ground sweet red peppers and gives food a great colour. Even though it looks like chilli powder, it isn't hot in flavour. You can also buy smoked paprika, which has a stronger taste and comes in mild and hot.

YAM
This vegetable tastes a bit like potatoes, and you can use it in the same way – mash or boil it, fry or bake as chips and balls. It comes in different shapes and colours, but I usually use the type with a tough brown outer skin and cream or white centre. Look for it in world food markets.

RICE
At the heart of Caribbean food is a good bowl of rice, especially the classic Rice 'n' Peas. I use basmati rice in this book – brown and white.

SCOTCH BONNET CHILLI
I love chilli hot food and the Scotch bonnet is hot! To make the chilli less spicy use it whole and add to a dish halfway through cooking, or you can remove the seeds but make sure you wear gloves or wash your hands afterwards!

SPRING ONIONS
These have a milder taste than regular onions and are used to add flavour and colour to many Caribbean dishes. They are also called scallions.

SWEET POTATO
They come in cream, purple and yellow, but my go-to sweet potato is orange inside. Baked whole, added to stews, or mashed – I love it!

TURMERIC
This spice adds a bright yellow colour to stews, curries and patties. It's also really good for you!

THYME
I like to use this herb fresh and dried in lots of different dishes, from jerk seasoning and curries to stews and bakes.

LIGHT BITES!

MILD

Serves 4-6
Takes 10 minutes

WHAT YOU NEED:

400g tin chickpeas,
drained

1 tablespoon extra-virgin
olive oil, plus extra to serve

50g tahini

Juice of 1 small lemon

1 garlic clove, peeled

all-purpose seasoning,
for sprinkling

Salt & black pepper

HAPPY HUMMUS

This tasty hummus is so easy to make and is
dipalicious scooped up on some toasted pitta or
vegetable sticks.

1 Drain the chickpeas (saving the liquid from the tin) and tip
them into a food processor or blender.

2 Add the olive oil, tahini, lemon juice and garlic and a good
pinch of salt and pepper, then blend until smooth and creamy. If
the hummus is too thick to blend, add some of the saved liquid
from the drained tin of chickpeas – I used about 4 tablespoons.

3 Spoon the hummus into a bowl and drizzle over a little extra
olive oil. Add a sprinkle of all-purpose seasoning, if you like.
Now tuck in… dunk vegetable sticks and pitta bread into the
hummus.

TAKE CARE…
Always ask an adult for help when using a sharp knife or
peeler, kitchen appliances and the hot oven or hob.

DID YOU KNOW?

Chickpeas have been used in cooking since ancient times by the Egyptians, Greeks and Romans.

DID YOU KNOW?
Tomatoes are a fruit not a vegetable as they contain seeds – even though they are used as a vegetable!

MEDIUM

Serves 4-6
Takes 20 minutes

WHAT YOU NEED:

1 tablespoon extra-virgin
olive oil, plus extra to serve

1 onion, finely chopped

1 large garlic clove,
finely chopped

2 red jalapeno chillies,
deseeded and finely chopped
(optional)

400g tin chopped tomatoes

½–1 tsp all-purpose
seasoning, or to taste

Juice of ½ lime

Handful of fresh coriander
leaves, chopped

Salt & black pepper

SALSA TIME

This tomato dip contains a tasty blend of herbs, spices and chilli. It can be hot so go carefully if you don't like chilli. Personally, I love it! Dunk in tortilla chips for a top snack.

1 Heat the oil in a saucepan over a medium heat. Add the finely chopped onion and cook, stirring occasionally, for 6 minutes until softened. Add the finely chopped garlic and jalapeño chilli, if using, and cook for another 1 minute, stirring.

2 Tip in the chopped tomatoes and all-purpose seasoning – add the smaller amount if you prefer a little chilli heat or add more if you like things a bit hot – and simmer over a low heat for 5 minutes, stirring occasionally, until reduced and thickened a little.

3 Spoon the salsa into a bowl (or you can blend it if you like a smooth salsa) and stir in the lime juice and coriander leaves. Season with salt and pepper, to taste. Spoon into a serving bowl and serve with tortilla chips.

MILD

Serves 4-6
Takes 20 minutes

NICELY CHEESY DIP

You won't believe this dip doesn't contain cheese! I like to top it with chopped fresh tomatoes and dunk in tortilla chips.

WHAT YOU NEED:

400g tin butter beans, drained and rinsed

50g vegan butter

1 garlic clove, crushed

1–2 red jalapeño chillies, deseeded and finely chopped (optional)

80ml oat milk

4 tablespoons nutritional yeast flakes

½–1 teaspoon dried chilli flakes (optional)

1 teaspoon onion powder

1 teaspoon smoked paprika

1 teaspoon ground cumin

1 teaspoon lemon juice

Salt & black pepper

1 Put the drained and rinsed butter beans in a saucepan with the vegan butter, garlic and jalapeño chilli, if using, and warm gently over a medium-low heat until the butter melts. Stir the mixture occasionally.

2 Add the nutritional yeast flakes, onion powder, oat milk, smoked paprika, cumin and dried chilli flakes, if using, and cook over a medium-low heat for 5 minutes, stirring, until reduced and thickened slightly.

3 Tip the bean mixture into a blender or use an electric hand blender. Add the lemon juice and blend until smooth and creamy. It should be like a thick sauce – add another tablespoon of oat milk if it is too thick to blend.

4 Spoon the dip into a bowl and season with salt and pepper, to taste. It is best served warm.

WHAT YOU NEED:

1 banana, peeled and
cut into chunks

½ mango, peeled, stone
removed and diced

1 passion fruit,
cut in half

300ml tropical fruit juice

RISING SUN FRUIT PUNCH

Refreshing and fruity – this is delicious served chilled on a hot day! Freezing the banana first makes it extra creamy and super-chilled, but you don't have to do this if you're in a hurry.

1 Put the banana chunks on a baking tray and freeze for about 1 hour until firmed up (this is optional).

2 Peel the mango using a vegetable peeler, then cut away the fruit around the large stone in the middle.

3 Scoop out the passion fruit with a teaspoon.

4 Put the banana, mango, passion fruit and tropical juice in a blender and blend until smooth – there may be a few seedy bits so strain it through a sieve if you prefer. Pour into two glasses and enjoy!

MUMMA BEAR SMOOTHIE

If it's a hot day, I like to put the ingredients for this fruit smoothie in the freezer first, just so everything is nice and chilled.

1 Put the banana chunks into a blender with the rest of the ingredients. Blend until everything is smooth and creamy.

2 Pour into two glasses and add straws.

WHAT YOU NEED:

2 bananas, peeled and cut into chunks

100g blackberries

300ml coconut drinking milk

100g strawberries, hulled

1 tablespoon maple syrup

DID YOU KNOW?
Coconut is the fruit (even though it's called a nut!) of the coconut palm, which is known as the 'tree of life'.

GO-GO ENERGY SMOOTHIE

This smoothie contains spinach, though you really wouldn't know it! It makes a great energy-boosting start to the day.

WHAT YOU NEED:

1 large banana, peeled and cut into chunks

150g tinned or fresh pineapple pieces

2 teaspoons hulled hemp seeds

1 large handful baby spinach leaves, stalks removed

300ml coconut drinking milk

1 Put the banana chunks and pineapple on a baking tray and freeze for about 1 hour until firmed up (this is optional).

2 Take the banana and pineapple out of the freezer and place in a blender with the rest of the ingredients. Blend everything until smooth and creamy. Pour into two glasses and drink straight away while it's still cool.

LUNCH TIME!

MILD

Serves 4
Takes 25 minutes

WHAT YOU NEED:

1 tablespoon olive oil

2 large leeks, sliced

2 garlic cloves, chopped

3 white potatoes, about 550g, peeled and chopped

1 teaspoon mild curry powder

1 teaspoon all-purpose seasoning'

½ teaspoon turmeric powder

1 vegetable stock cube

200ml oat milk

Salt & black pepper

LEEK & POTATO SOUP

This popular vegetable soup has been given a spicy twist with the addition of mild curry powder and turmeric. If spices aren't your thing you can leave them out.

1 Heat the olive oil in a large saucepan over a medium heat. Stir in the sliced leeks and cook, stirring often, for 5 minutes until nice and soft.

2 Add the chopped garlic, chopped potatoes, curry powder, all-purpose seasoning and turmeric and give it a good stir.

3 Crumble the vegetable stock cube into 1 litre of just-boiled water from the kettle, stir and pour it into the pan.

4 Bring the stock to the boil, then turn the heat down to low. Part-cover the pan with a lid and simmer for 10 minutes or until the potatoes are soft.

5 Pour in the oat milk and warm through briefly.

6 Blend using an electric hand blender until smooth and creamy. Season with salt and pepper to taste. Now it's time to serve the soup with roti or your favourite bread.

DID YOU KNOW?

Turmeric has been used for centuries in traditional Indian medicine for its anti-inflammatory properties thanks to an ingredient called curcumin.

CHILLI ALERT!

Makes 6
Takes 1.5 hours,
plus chilling

WHAT YOU NEED:

For the pastry:

240g plain flour

1 ½ tablespoons turmeric powder

½ teaspoon salt

1 teaspoon curry powder

120g vegan butter, cut into small pieces, chilled

For the filling:

1 tablespoon olive oil

4 spring onions, chopped

3 garlic cloves, finely chopped

180g chilled or frozen vegan mince

½ Scotch bonnet, deseeded and finely chopped (optional)

½ teaspoon ground allspice

1 teaspoon ground cumin

1 teaspoon dried thyme

2 tablespoons coconut drinking milk

60g frozen peas

1 teaspoon jerk marinade

2 tablespoons tomato purée

60g tinned sweetcorn

3 tablespoons vegan butter, melted

Salt & black pepper

JAMAICAN PATTIES

This vegan version of the famous Jamaican patty is delicious – who needs meat!

1 To make the pastry, mix together the flour, turmeric, curry powder and salt in a large mixing bowl. Using your fingertips, rub the vegan butter into the flour mixture until it looks like breadcrumbs. Gradually stir in about 3 tablespoons ice-cold water using a fork and then your fingers until the mixture comes together into a ball of dough. Wrap in cling film and chill for 30 minutes.

2 Meanwhile, heat the olive oil in a large frying pan over a medium heat. Add the chopped spring onions and finely chopped garlic and cook, stirring occasionally, for 1 minute until soft. Add the mince, Scotch bonnet, ground allspice, onion powder and thyme and cook for 5 minutes, stirring to break up the mince.

3 Add the coconut milk, and tomato puree and jerk marinade then stir in the peas and sweetcorn and cook for 5 minutes until the peas are tender. Season with salt and pepper and carefully tip the mixture into a bowl and leave to cool.

4 Preheat the oven to 180°C/350°F/Gas 4. Line a large baking tray with baking paper.

5 To make the patties, unwrap the pastry and divide into 6 equal-size pieces. Roll out one of the pieces on a lightly floured work surface into a 15cm diameter round, about 5mm thick. Wet the rim of the pastry with a finger dipped in water. Place 2 heaped tablespoons of the filling mixture on the bottom half of the pastry near the middle. Fold the pastry over the filling into a half-moon shape. Use a fork to seal the edges and prick the top 3 times.

6 Place the patty on the lined baking tray and repeat to make 6 in total. Brush the tops of the patties with melted butter and bake for 35 minutes until the pastry is cooked and golden. Leave to cool a little, then tuck in.

Serves 4
Takes 35 minutes

WHAT YOU NEED:

3 tablespoons olive oil

1 onion, chopped

2 carrots, peeled and diced

1 red pepper, deseeded and chopped

1–2 garlic cloves, crushed

½ teaspoon thyme

1 tomato, chopped

2 x 280g tins callaloo, drained and rinsed

100g baby spinach leaves

½ teaspoon paprika

1 teaspoon all-purpose seasoning

1 Scotch bonnet chilli (leave whole) (optional)

Salt & black pepper

CALLALOO MIX-UP

Callaloo is a good-for-you leafy green vegetable, a bit like spinach, and is also the name of a popular dish in Caribbean cooking. My version is a bit like a Jamaican stir-fry!

1 Heat the oil in a large, deep frying pan with a lid over a medium heat. Add the chopped onion and cook, stirring often, for 5 minutes until softened.

2 Add the diced carrots and chopped red pepper and cook, stirring often, for 5 minutes until softened.

3 Next, add the garlic, thyme, tomato, callaloo, spinach, paprika, all-purpose seasoning, Scotch bonnet chilli, if using, and 2 tablespoons water. Turn the heat down a little and cover the pan with a lid. Cook, stirring occasionally, for 7–10 minutes until the vegetables are tender. Add a splash more water if it looks too dry. Season with salt and pepper to taste.

4 Now is the time to serve the callaloo – you can eat it with bread, rice, fried dumplings or boiled hard food (dumpling, banana and yam). It also makes a great side dish.

Serves 4
Takes 30 minutes, plus chilling

WHAT YOU NEED:

2 sweet potatoes, about 400g, peeled and chopped

2 tablespoons sunflower oil, plus extra for frying

1 small red onion, finely chopped

2 spring onions, thinly sliced

2 garlic cloves, chopped

1 teaspoon jerk marinade

1 teaspoon all-purpose seasoning

400g tin chickpeas, drained

75g breadcrumbs

Flour, for coating your hands

Salt & black pepper

SWEET POTATO & CHICKPEA BURGERS

These spicy burgers are the best – serve in a bun with your favourite sauces, relishes and salad.

1 Microwave the sweet potatoes on medium-high for 6 minutes or until tender when pierced with a skewer (or bake them at 200°C/400°F/Gas 6 for 50 minutes).

2 Meanwhile, heat the oil in a large frying pan over a medium heat. Add the finely chopped onion and thinly sliced spring onions and cook, stirring often, for 5 minutes until softened.

3 Add the chopped garlic, jerk marinade and all-purpose seasoning and cook for another 1 minute. Spoon the mixture into a large bowl and leave to cool.

4 Tip the chickpeas into a bowl and mash with the back of a fork to a crumbly mixture.

5 When the sweet potato is ready, cut each one in half and scoop out the middle with a spoon. Roughly mash the sweet potato and tip into the bowl with the fried onion mixture. Stir in the mashed chickpeas until everything is mixed together and season with salt and pepper to taste. Leave to cool.

6 Tip the breadcrumbs onto a plate.

7 Shape the sweet potato mixture into 4 burgers with floured hands. Dunk them into the breadcrumbs until coated on both sides. Place on a plate and chill for 30 minutes to firm up.

8 Pour enough oil to generously coat the bottom of a large frying pan over a medium heat. Cook the burgers for 5 minutes on each side until golden and crisp. Serve in a burger bun with all your favourite extras!

MILD

Serves 4
Takes 40 minutes

WHAT YOU NEED:

1 tablespoon
olive oil

1 onion,
finely chopped

2 garlic cloves,
finely chopped

1cm piece fresh
ginger, peeled and
finely chopped

1–2 teaspoons
garam masala

¼–½ teaspoon
mild chilli powder
(optional)

1 potato, about 200g,
peeled and diced

1 carrot, peeled
and diced

200g chilled or frozen
vegan mince

2 tablespoons
tomato purée

100g frozen
peas

4 soft flour
tortillas, to serve

1 handful of grated
vegan cheese

Salt & black
pepper

SPICY VEGETABLE WRAPS

I've given these wraps a mild chilli rating, but it is virtually medium so take it easy if you don't like chilli! Top the wrap with shredded lettuce, if you like.

1 Heat the oil in a large frying pan with a lid over a medium heat. Add the finely chopped onion and cook, stirring often, for 5 minutes until softened.

2 Add the finely chopped garlic and ginger and cook, stirring, for another 1 minute.

3 Stir in the garam masala, chilli powder, if using, the diced potato, diced carrot, vegan mince, tomato purée and 150ml water. Stir well, breaking up the mince with the back of a fork. When the mixture starts to bubble, turn the heat to low and cover with a lid. Simmer, stirring occasionally, for 10–15 minutes until the potato and carrot are tender.

4 Add the frozen peas and cook for 3 minutes until tender. Taste and season with salt and pepper, if needed.

5 Meanwhile, wrap the tortillas in foil and warm in a low oven.

6 Spoon the mince mixture on one half of each tortilla. Top with the grated vegan cheese (you could also add some shredded lettuce). Serve the tortillas open or rolled up, tucking in the ends, then cut in half before serving. Enjoy!

DID YOU KNOW?
Ginger may help to fight germs in the body and
is good for our digestive systems.

CHILLI ALERT!

Serves 4
Takes 40 minutes

ACKEE & HEARTS OF PALM

This is my vegan version of the traditional Caribbean dish of ackee and salt fish – I think it's just as good!

WHAT YOU NEED:

400g tin hearts of palm, drained and shredded

1 tablespoon vegan fish seasoning or light soy sauce

2 tablespoons olive oil

1 onion, chopped

2 peppers (green and red), deseeded and chopped

1 Scotch bonnet chilli, left whole, or 1 jalapeño chilli, deseeded and chopped (optional)

2 garlic cloves, finely chopped

2 spring onions, chopped

5 tomatoes, chopped

1 teaspoon all-purpose seasoning

2 teaspoons fresh thyme leaves

540g tin ackee, drained

1 handful of parsley leaves, chopped

Salt & black pepper

1 Put the hearts of palm in a bowl and pull apart into long strips. Pour over the fish sauce, turn until coated and leave to marinate while you prepare the rest of the dish.

2 Meanwhile, heat the oil in a large, deep frying pan over a medium heat. Add the chopped onion and cook, stirring occasionally, for 5 minutes, until softened.

3 Add the chopped green and red peppers and cook for another 5 minutes until tender.

4 Add the garlic, Scotch bonnet chilli, if using, spring onions, tomatoes, all-purpose seasoning and thyme and cook for another 2 minutes until softened.

5 Add the ackee and hearts of palm with the vegan fish sauce and stir gently until combined. Season with salt and pepper and heat through, stirring. Take out the chilli. Spoon onto a serving plate and scatter over the parsley – enjoy your lunch!

Take care...

Only use the Scotch bonnet chilli if you like lots of heat – it's very hot! You could use a milder tasting chilli instead, like a jalapeño, or leave it out altogether. It's a good idea to wear rubber gloves when chopping up chilli and make sure you don't touch your face after cutting it.

 **MEDIUM**

Serves 4
Takes 1 hour

WHAT YOU NEED:

400g tin jackfruit, drained

1 tablespoon olive oil

1 onion, chopped

2 garlic cloves, crushed

1 teaspoon dried thyme

1 teaspoon all-purpose seasoning

1 teaspoon jerk marinade

4 tablespoons of your favourite barbecue sauce

200ml tin chopped tomatoes

2 teaspoons white wine vinegar

Salt & black pepper

BBQ JACKFRUIT

Jackfruit makes a great vegan alternative to meat. Look for it in tins packed in water, not syrup, for this recipe. Some say it tastes just like pulled pork when cooked in a barbecue sauce!

1 Remove the seeds from the tinned jackfruit and cut any large pieces in half.

2 Heat the oil in a saucepan over a medium heat. Add the chopped onion and cook, stirring often, for 5 minutes until softened. Add the crushed garlic and cook for another 1 minute.

3 Add the thyme, all-purpose seasoning and jerk marinade, stir, then add the jackfruit, barbecue sauce, vinegar, chopped tomatoes and 150ml water. When the sauce starts to bubble turn the heat to low, cover with a lid, and simmer for 30 minutes. Stir the sauce every now and then to stop it sticking to the bottom of the pan.

4 Take the lid off and cook for another 5 minutes until the sauce has reduced and thickened.

5 Preheat the oven to 220°C/425°F/Gas 7. Line a large baking tray with baking paper.

6 Spoon the jackfruit onto the lined baking tray. Now the fun bit! Using two forks, pull the jackfruit into strips, so it looks shredded. Add a splash of water to the sauce in the pan and spoon it over the shredded jackfruit until coated. Place in the oven for 15 minutes until starting to crisp at the edges.

7 I like to spoon the jackfruit on top of tortillas, with any spare sauce, and top with chopped avocado, tomato, coleslaw and some fresh coriander. A spoonful of dairy-free crème fraîche and salsa is great, too.

MEDIUM

Serves 4
Takes 50 minutes

WHAT YOU NEED:

100g plain flour

1 teaspoon jerk spice mix

½ teaspoon garlic powder

175ml oat milk

1 whole cauliflower, leaves removed, broken into large bite-size florets

½–1 teaspoon hot sauce, to taste (it's pretty hot!)

1 tablespoon maple syrup

1 teaspoon sunflower oil

Salt & black pepper

HOT CAULI BITES

These cauli florets are dipped in a spiced batter and baked in the oven until golden. They're delicious dunked into dairy-free mayo – I also like to add a spoonful of sweet chilli sauce.

1 To make the batter, mix together the plain flour, jerk spice mix, garlic powder and oat milk in a large mixing bowl. Season with salt and pepper.

2 Preheat the oven to 190°C/375°F/Gas 5. Line a large baking tray with baking paper.

3 Dip the cauliflower florets, one at a time, into the thick, spicy batter until coated all over. Let them drip a little over the bowl to remove any excess batter, then place them slightly spaced apart on the lined baking tray.

4 Bake for 20 minutes, turning once, until light golden all over and the batter sets.

5 Meanwhile, mix together the hot sauce, maple syrup and sunflower oil.

6 Carefully remove the baking tray from the oven. Brush the hot sauce mixture over the cauliflower bites until coated, then put the tray back in the oven for another 20 minutes until golden. Place in a serving bowl then tuck in, dunking them into a sweet chilli mayo, if you like.

WHAT YOU NEED:

For the base:

350g self-raising
flour

½ teaspoon
baking powder

1 teaspoon
salt

2 tablespoons plain
vegan yogurt

1 tablespoon extra-virgin olive
oil, plus extra for drizzling

For the topping:

150g passata

1 tablespoon tomato
purée

1 teaspoon dried
oregano

1 teaspoon garlic
powder

1 small red
onion, thinly
sliced into rings

1 red pepper,
deseeded
and sliced

100g tinned or fresh
pineapple
pieces

150g vegan
mozzarella cheese,
torn into small pieces

Black pepper

1 handful of
basil leaves

MY TROPICAL PIZZA

I've used a quick, yeast-free pizza base that doesn't need time to rise so it's perfect for lunchtime. Feel free to add your own favourite toppings.

1 First make the pizza base, mix together the flour, baking powder and salt in a large bowl. Stir in the yogurt, olive oil and 140ml water, first with a fork and then with your hands until it comes together into a slightly sticky ball of dough.

2 Now it's time to get your hands messy, tip the dough onto a lightly floured work surface and knead for a few seconds into a soft ball of dough. Add another 1 tablespoon flour if it is too sticky. Shape your dough into a ball and leave it to sit for 15 minutes, covered.

3 Preheat the oven to 220°C/425°F/Gas 7. Sprinkle flour over a large baking tray.

4 Meanwhile, prepare the topping ingredients. To make the tomato sauce, mix together the passata, tomato purée, oregano and garlic powder in a bowl, then season with salt and pepper to taste.

5 Roll out the dough on a lightly floured work surface the same size as the baking tray, keeping the edges slightly thicker than the middle.

6 Spread the tomato sauce over the dough, leaving a border around the edge.

7 Now have fun with the toppings! Scatter over the pineapple pieces, sliced red onion, sliced red pepper and mozzarella. Drizzle over a little olive oil and bake for 16–18 minutes until the base is cooked and the top lovely and melted and bubbling. Scatter over a few basil leaves, cut into wedges and dig in.

DID YOU KNOW?

A pineapple can take nearly 2 years to grow!

MUSHROOM QUINOA SPECIAL

Who doesn't love a stir-fry? This mushoom one is a favourite and comes with super-healthy quinoa. Noodles or rice are good alternatives, too.

WHAT YOU NEED:

180g multi-coloured quinoa, rinsed

425ml vegetable stock

2 tablespoons olive oil

1 onion, chopped

4 spring onions, thinly slice

3 garlic cloves, chopped

1 orange pepper, deseeded and chopped

400g chestnut mushrooms, roughly chopped

12 cherry tomatoes, halved

1 teaspoon dried oregano

1 teaspoon all-purpose seasoning

1 handful of basil leaves, torn (optional)

Salt & black pepper

1 Put the quinoa in a saucepan and pour over the vegetable stock. Bring to the boil, then turn the heat down to low, cover with a lid, and simmer for 12–15 minutes until the water has been absorbed. Turn off the heat and leave the quinoa to sit until needed.

2 Meanwhile, heat the oil in a large frying pan over a medium heat. Add the chopped onion and cook, stirring occasionally, for 5 minutes until softened.

3 Add most of the spring onions, saving some of the green parts to scatter over at the end. Stir in the chopped garlic, chopped orange pepper and the chopped mushrooms. Stir-fry over a medium-high heat for 8 minutes until the mushrooms start to turn golden.

4 Add the halved cherry tomatoes, oregano, all-purpose seasoning and 2 tablespoons water and cook for another 5 minutes, stirring until the tomatoes start to break down. Season with salt and pepper to taste.

5 Spoon the quinoa into four serving bowls and top with the mushroom stir fry. Finish with a scattering of basil leaves, if using, and the saved green bits of the spring onions.

DIN DIN!

DID YOU KNOW?
Red peppers are ripe green peppers.
They taste sweeter as they ripen.

Serves 4
Takes 1.5 hours

COTTAGE PIE

We all love cottage pie and this vegan version goes down really well in my family.

WHAT YOU NEED:

2 tablespoons olive oil

1 onion, chopped

2 carrots, peeled and cut into small pieces

1 red pepper, deseeded and cut into small chunks

2 large garlic cloves, finely chopped

1 teaspoon all-purpose seasoning

1 teaspoon dried thyme

400g chilled or frozen vegan mince

1 tin chopped tomatoes

1 tablespoon tomato ketchup

1 tablespoon jerk marinade

250ml vegetable stock

800g white potatoes, peeled and cut into large chunks

350g sweet potatoes, peeled and cut into large chunks

50g vegan butter, cut into pieces

3–5 tablespoons oat milk

Salt & black pepper

Peas or your favourite green veg, to serve

1 To make the mince part of the cottage pie, heat the olive oil in a saucepan over a medium heat. Add the chopped onion, chopped carrots and chopped red pepper and cook, stirring often, for 7 minutes until softened.

2 Add the garlic, all-purpose seasoning and thyme and cook over for another 1 minute.

3 Pour in the chopped tomatoes, ketchup, jerk marinade and stock.

4 While the mince mixture is cooking, prepare the mashed potato topping. Put the white potatoes and sweet potatoes in a large pan and pour over enough cold water to cover. Bring to the boil over a high heat, then turn the heat down a little and cook the potatoes for 12–15 minutes until soft. Carefully drain the potatoes, asking an adult to help you, then put them back in the pan to dry off.

5 Add the vegan butter and 3 tablespoons oat milk and mash with a potato masher until smooth. Add more oat milk if needed, then season with salt and pepper, to taste. Meanwhile, preheat the oven to 200°C/400°F/Gas 6.

6 Spoon the mince mixture into 4 individual ovenproof dishes or 1 large dish, then spoon the mash on top and spread out evenly with the back of a spoon. Rough up the mash with a fork and dot extra butter on top. Bake for 40 minutes, or until the top is golden. Serve with peas or your favourite green veg.

MEDIUM

Serves 4
Takes 45 minutes

WHAT YOU NEED:

1 tablespoon
vegetable oil

1 onion,
chopped

1 red pepper,
deseeded and
chopped

3 white potatoes,
about 450g, peeled and
cut into bite-size chunks

3 carrots, peeled
and cubed

400g tin
chickpeas, drained

2.5cm piece fresh
ginger, peeled
and finely grated

2 garlic cloves,
finely chopped

1 tablespoon fresh
thyme leaves

1 teaspoon
all-purpose seasoning

1–2 tablespoons
mild curry powder

1 vegetable
stock cube

1 tablespoon
tomato purée

Salt &
black pepper

CHICKPEA CURRY

This is made with storecupboard ingredients so is super easy. I also like to add sweet potatoes, but I've kept things simple here. Serve with rice, roti or flatbreads.

1 Heat the oil in a saucepan over a medium heat. Add the chopped onion and chopped red pepper and cook, stirring occasionally, for 5 minutes until softened.

2 Stir in the potato chunks, sliced carrots, chickpeas, grated ginger, finely chopped garlic, thyme, all-purpose seasoning and curry powder and cook for another 2 minutes.

3 Meanwhile, crumble the stock cube into 500ml of just-boiled water until it dissolves. Stir in the tomato puree.

4 Pour the stock into the pan and give everything a good mix. When it starts to bubble turn the heat down to medium-low, cover the pan with a lid and simmer for 15–20 minutes until the vegetables are tender when pierced with a fork. Season with salt and pepper to taste. Serve sprinkled with a little extra fresh thyme, if you like, with rice, roti or flatbreads.

DID YOU KNOW?

Pasta can contain egg, which is not vegan-friendly, so do make sure you buy egg-free lasagne sheets.

Serves 4
Takes 1 hour,
45 minutes

WHAT YOU NEED:

2 tablespoons
olive oil

1 onion, roughly
chopped

1 red pepper,
deseeded and
chopped

4 garlic cloves,
finely chopped

400g chilled or
frozen vegan mince

600g jar
passata

1 teaspoon
ground cumin

1 teaspoon all-purpose
seasoning

½ teaspoon
ground allspice

1 teaspoon
dried thyme

Salt &
black pepper

6 egg-free dried
lasagne sheets,
about 125g

For the 'cheesy' sauce:

50g vegan
butter

50g plain
flour

500ml almond
milk, warmed

¼ teaspoon
ground nutmeg

3 tablespoons nutritional
yeast flakes

MY SPECIAL LASAGNE

As you know I like spices, so it's no surprise that my recipe for lasagne contains a few just to liven things up a bit! Serve it with a salad or veg.

1 Heat the olive oil in a saucepan over a medium heat. Add the chopped onion and cook, stirring, for 5 minutes until softened.

2 Add the chopped red pepper and finely chopped garlic and cook for another 5 minutes, stirring often, until softened.

3 Stir in the vegan mince, passata, cumin, all-purpose seasoning, allspice, thyme and 50ml water and when the sauce starts to bubble, turn down the heat slightly. Part-cover the pan with a lid and cook for 20 minutes until reduced and thickened. Stir the sauce occasionally so it doesn't stick. Season with salt and pepper to taste.

4 Meanwhile, make the 'cheesy' white sauce. Melt the vegan butter over a low heat in a small pan. Using a small balloon whisk, gradually stir in the flour. Cook, stirring, over a low heat for 1 minute until it makes a light brown paste. Gradually, pour in the warm almond milk and cook for 5 minutes, stirring, until thickened. Stir in the nutmeg and nutritional yeast flakes.

5 Preheat the oven to 200°C/400°F/Gas 6.

6 Now it's time to put together the lasagne – you will need a deep ovenproof dish, about 22 x 15cm. Spoon a third of the vegan mince mixture in the bottom of the dish. Top with a layer of lasagne, breaking the sheets if needed so the mince is covered. Spoon another layer of vegan mince on top followed by half the 'cheesy' sauce. Now for another layer of lasagne sheets and the remaining vegan mince. Finish with a third layer of lasagne sheets and the rest of the 'cheesy' sauce.

7 Bake the lasagne for 40–45 minutes until the top starts to bubble and turn golden. Now tuck in!

MEDIUM

Serves 4
20 minutes

WHAT YOU NEED:

3 courgettes,
ends trimmed
and spiralized

2 tablespoons
olive oil

4 spring onions,
thinly sliced

300g cherry
tomatoes, halved

175g canned
sweetcorn, drained

280g vegan
'chicken' pieces

1 handful of sugar
snap peas, halved
diagonally

2 garlic cloves,
finely chopped

½ teaspoon
dried oregano

1 teaspoon all-purpose
seasoning

½–1 teaspoon
jerk spice mix

1 handful of fresh
basil leaves
(optional)

Vegan parmesan,
grated, to serve
(optional)

Salt & black
pepper

ZOODLENESE

Ask your mum or dad to get you a spiralizer – they're so fun and useful too; you can spiralize lots of different vegetables! Here, spiralized courgettes make a great stir-fry.

1 Put the spiralized courgettes in a bowl and set aside for later.

2 Heat the olive oil in a large wok or frying pan over medium-high heat. Add the thinly sliced spring onions, halved cherry tomatoes, sweetcorn, vegan 'chicken' pieces and sugar snap peas and stir-fry for 3 minutes.

3 Add the garlic, oregano, all-purpose seasoning, jerk spice and 120ml water and stir-fry for another 1 minutes.

4 Now tip in the spiralized courgettes and stir-fry for 1 minute or until slightly softened – you want them to keep their shape and colour. Season with salt and pepper to taste.

5 Spoon into bowls and top with basil leaves and vegan parmesan, if you like. Dig in!

DID YOU KNOW?
Courgettes, known as zucchini in the US, are about 95 per cent water!

Serves 4
Takes 45 minutes

WHAT YOU NEED:

2 tablespoons
sunflower oil

1 onion,
chopped

1 red pepper,
deseeded and
chopped

1 green pepper,
deseeded and
chopped

4 garlic cloves,
finely chopped

1 teaspoon
ground allspice

½ teaspoon
turmeric powder

1 teaspoon all-purpose
seasoning

1 tablespoon fresh
thyme leaves

2 sweet potatoes,
about 450g, peeled
and cut into
bite-size chunks

450g butternut
squash, peeled,
deseeded and cut
into bite-size chunks

1 teaspoon all-purpose
200ml
vegetable stock

400g tin
coconut milk

1 Scotch bonnet,
left whole, or jalapeño
chilli, deseeded and
chopped (optional)

100g tinned
callaloo or
spinach leaves

1 corn-on-the-cob,
kernals sliced off,
or 175g canned
sweetcorn

Salt & black
pepper

ITAL RUNDOWN

Traditionally, 'Ital' food means one-pot cooking in Jamaica and other parts of the Caribbean. This veggie stew is based on a typical dish and also includes coconut milk.

1 Heat the oil in a saucepan over a medium heat. Add the chopped onion and cook, stirring occasionally, for 5 minutes until softened.

2 Add the chopped red pepper and green pepper and finely chopped garlic and cook for another 3 minutes, stirring often.

3 Stir in the allspice, turmeric, all-purpose seasoning, thyme, sweet potato and butternut squash chunks.

4 Pour in the vegetable stock and coconut milk and add the whole Scotch bonnet or chopped chilli, if using. I like my rundown hot, but you don't need to use chilli if it's not your thing! Bring to the boil, then turn the heat down to medium-low. Cover with a lid and simmer gently, stirring occasionally, for 10 minutes.

5 Add the callaloo or spinach and sweetcorn and cook for another 5–10 minutes until all the vegetables are tender. Take care that the Scotch bonnet doesn't burst when stirring or it will make everything very hot! Season with salt and pepper, then tuck in. I like to serve it with rice.

WHAT YOU NEED:

1 tablespoon
olive oil

1 onion,
chopped

1 red pepper,
deseeded and
chopped

250g chestnut
mushrooms,
sliced

2 garlic cloves,
finely chopped

400g lentils,
rinsed

1 teaspoon
ground allspice

1 tablespoon fresh
thyme leaves

1 teaspoon
all-purpose
seasoning

400g tin
chopped
tomatoes

2 bay
leaves

600ml
vegetable stock

2 tablespoons
tomato purée

400g dried egg-
free spaghetti

vegan parmesan,
grated, to serve

Salt & black
pepper

LENTIL BOLOGNESE

Who needs meat, when you have lentils! This is a favourite weekday meal in my family. Serve it with some green veg.

1 Heat the olive oil in a saucepan over a medium heat. Add the chopped onion and cook, stirring occasionally, for 5 minutes until softened.

2 Add the chopped red pepper, sliced mushrooms and finely chopped garlic and cook for 10 minutes until softened.

3 Stir in the lentils, allspice, all-purpose seasoning, thyme, bay leaves, chopped tomatoes, tomato puree and stock. When the sauce starts to bubble, turn the heat down a little. Part-cover the pan with a lid and simmer for 40 minutes, stirring occasionally, until the lentils are cooked. Season with salt and pepper to taste.

4 About 15 minutes before the bolognese sauce is ready, bring a large pan of salted water to the boil. Add the pasta, stir, and cook for 10–12 minutes until just tender. Carefully drain the pasta, asking an adult to help you, and divide between four shallow bowls or plates. Spoon the sauce on top and serve with a sprinkling of vegan parmesan.

DID YOU KNOW?

Lentils are nutritious and cheap to buy. Made up of over 25 per cent protein, they make a good meat substitute.

DID YOU KNOW?

Eating vegetables every day is good for your health. Make sure
you eat a range of different coloured ones.

 **MEDIUM**

Serves 4
**Takes 1 hour,
20 minutes**

WHAT YOU NEED:

400g tin
chopped
tomatoes

1 tablespoon olive
oil, plus extra
for drizzling

2 garlic cloves,
finely chopped

1 onion,
chopped

1 red pepper,
deseeded and
thickly sliced

1 teaspoon
dried thyme

1 teaspoon
all-purpose
seasoning

1 teaspoon
jerk marinade

1 sweet potato,
peeled, cut in half
and cut into ½cm
thick slices

1 yellow pepper,
deseeded and
thickly sliced

1 orange pepper,
deseeded and
cut into chunks

250g butternut
squash, peeled,
deseeded and cut
into ½cm thick slices

2 courgettes,
sliced

Salt & black
pepper

McQUEEN RATATOUILLE

This is a step up from your regular ratatouille! The veg are roasted in a great-tasting, spicy red pepper and tomato sauce.

1 Put the chopped tomatoes, oil, garlic, onion, red pepper, thyme, all-purpose seasoning and jerk marinade in a blender and blend until almost smooth. Season with salt and pepper, to taste, and set aside.

2 Preheat the oven to 200°C/400°F/Gas 6.

3 Now's the time to get layering! Arrange an even layer of sweet potatoes in the bottom of a large ovenproof dish, about 34 x 28cm, and top with a third of the tomato sauce. Next add a layer of yellow and orange peppers and another third of the tomato sauce. Top with the butternut squash and the remaining tomato sauce. Finish with a layer of courgettes. Drizzle over some more olive oil and season with salt and pepper to taste.

4 Cover the dish with foil and bake for 45 minutes. Carefully take off the foil and cook for another 10 minutes or until the vegetables are tender and starting to turn golden on top. Serve with bread for dunking into the sauce.

MEDIUM

Serves 4
Takes 30 minutes

RASTA PASTA

This colourful pasta dish has a delicious creamy, cheesy sauce – and it's all dairy-free!

WHAT YOU NEED:

2 tablespoons olive oil

4 spring onions, thinly sliced

400g egg-free pasta swirls

1 yellow pepper, deseeded and cut into chunks

1 green pepper, deseeded and cut into chunks

1 red pepper, deseeded and cut into chunks

3 garlic cloves, finely chopped

1 teaspoon oregano

1 teaspoon all-purpose seasoning

1 teaspoon jerk marinade

250ml dairy-free crème fraiche

100g vegan mozzarella, thinly sliced

1 handful of fresh basil leaves (optional)

Salt & black pepper

50g vegan cheddar cheese, coarsely grated, to serve

1 Cook the pasta in a large saucepan of boiling salted water following the instructions on the packet.

2 Meanwhile, heat the olive oil in a large, deep frying pan over a medium heat. Add the sliced spring onions and the chopped yellow, green and red peppers and cook, stirring often, for 5 minutes until softened. Turn the heat down slightly if the vegetables start to turn brown. Stir in the finely chopped garlic, oregano, all-purpose seasoning and jerk marinade and cook for another 1 minute.

3 Turn the heat down to low. Spoon in the dairy-free crème fraîche and thinly sliced mozzarella and cook gently, stirring, for 5 minutes until you have a creamy sauce.

4 Your pasta should be ready now. Carefully drain it, asking an adult to help you, and save 200ml of the cooking water.

5 Stir the pasta cooking water into the creamy sauce, then season with salt and pepper to taste.

6 Add the cooked pasta and turn everything with a large spoon until the pasta is coated in the sauce. Now you're ready to serve. Top with a few basil leaves, if you like, and grated vegan cheddar for an extra cheesy hit.

DID YOU KNOW?
Peppers are actually fruits and come in a variety of colours – red, yellow, orange, green and purple.

DID YOU KNOW?

Butter beans, also known as lima beans, are named after their butter-like colour and creamy texture.

CHILLI ALERT

Serves 4
Takes 1 hour

WHAT YOU NEED:

2 tablespoons olive oil

1 onion, chopped

4 spring onions, chopped

3 garlic cloves, chopped

2 large carrots, quartered lengthways and cut into small chunks

350g butternut squash, peeled, deseeded and cut into small chunks

1 teaspoon all-purpose seasoning

1 teaspoon ground allspice

1 teaspoon dried thyme

1 teaspoon jerk marinade

400g tin butter beans, drained and rinsed

400g tin jackfruit, drained, pieces halved if large

1 tablespoon browning or soy sauce

600ml vegetable stock

1 tablespoon tomato ketchup

100g passata

1 Scotch bonnet chilli, left whole (optional)

Salt & black pepper

BROWN JACKFRUIT STEW

Brown stew is a typical dish eaten for dinner throughout the Caribbean. I've included jackfruit, vegetables and butter beans in my version.

1 Heat the olive oil in a large saucepan over a medium heat. Add the chopped onion and cook, stirring occasionally, for 5 minutes until softened.

2 Add the chopped spring onions, chopped garlic, chopped carrots and butternut squash chunks, and cook, stirring for another 5 minutes.

3 Stir in the all-purpose seasoning, allspice and thyme followed by the jerk marinade, jackfruit and butter beans.

4 Now mix in the browning or soy sauce, stock, tomato ketchup and passata. When the sauce starts to bubble, turn the heat down. Put the lid on and simmer for 25–30 minutes, stirring every so often, until the vegetables are cooked. Add the whole Scotch bonnet chilli halfway through cooking if you like it a bit hot, or you can leave it out! Take the lid off the stew if the sauce is too runny and you need to reduce the liquid.

5 When it's ready, season with salt and pepper and serve with some delicious plain rice or rice and peas (see page 82).

SWEET POTATO & SPINACH BAKE

This one-dish meal makes a simple and easy family dinner. Serve with extra veg on the side.

WHAT YOU NEED:

1 tablespoon
olive oil

2 onions,
thinly sliced

3 garlic cloves,
finely chopped

1 teaspoon
smoked paprika

1 teaspoon
ground cumin

1 teaspoon all-purpose
seasoning

2 teaspoons
plain flour

350ml coconut
drinking milk

200g spinach
leaves, stalks
removed

3 sweet potatoes,
about 900g, peeled
and thinly sliced

60g vegan
cheddar cheese,
coarsely grated

Salt & black
pepper

1 Preheat the oven to 200°C/400°F/Gas 6.

2 Heat the olive oil in a large, deep frying pan over a medium heat. Add the thinly sliced onion and cook for 9 minutes, stirring often, until softened. Add the finely chopped garlic and cook for another 1 minute.

3 Stir in the smoked paprika, cumin, all-purpose seasoning and flour and cook, stirring, for 1 minute.

4 Pour in the coconut drinking milk, turn the heat down and simmer, stirring, for 2–3 minutes until thickened slightly. Season with salt and pepper to taste.

5 Meanwhile, steam the spinach for 3 minutes until the leaves are tender. Mix the spinach into the coconut sauce.

6 Spoon a quarter of the sauce into a large ovenproof dish. Top with a layer of thinly sliced sweet potato. Spoon another layer of sauce and then more sweet potatoes. Repeat once more finishing with a final layer of sauce, so you have 3 layers of potato and 4 layers of sauce. Cover the dish with foil and bake for 50 minutes until the sweet potatoes are tender.

7 Carefully remove the dish from the oven. Take off the foil and scatter the vegan cheese over the top, then return to the oven for another 10 minutes until the cheese has melted.

DID YOU KNOW?
Sweet potatoes are a starchy
root vegetable that come in a variety of shapes
and colours, but I like the ones that are golden orange best.

DID YOU KNOW?
Tofu is made from soya beans
and is a good source of protein.

Serves 4
Takes 30 minutes,
plus marinating

WHAT YOU NEED:

2 tablespoons
olive oil

1 tablespoon
maple syrup

2 tablespoons
jerk marinade
or sauce

1 teaspoon
all-purpose
seasoning

200g smoked
tofu, cut into
16 x 1cm cubes

1 large yellow
pepper, deseeded
and cut into
16 chunks

2 red onions,
halved and cut
into 16 small
wedges

1 large red pepper,
deseeded and
cut into 16 chunks

2 courgettes,
cut into 16
thick slices

Salt &
black pepper

Lime wedges,
to serve

SIMPLE KEBABS

You can swap any of the vegetables for your own favourites, but a mix of colours looks best. These kebabs make great summer food, especially when cooked on the barbecue.

1 Soak 8 wooden kebab sticks in cold water for 30 minutes – this will stop them burning when cooking the kebabs.

2 Meanwhile, mix together 1 tablespoon of the olive oil, the all-purpose seasoning, jerk marinade or sauce and maple syrup in a shallow dish. Add the tofu to the dish, turn with a spoon until coated, then set aside for 30 minutes to let it soak up all the flavours of the marinade.

3 Put all the vegetables in a large mixing bowl. Pour over the remaining 1 tablespoon olive oil, season with salt and pepper and mix everything together with your hands until the vegetables are coated in the seasoned oil.

4 Preheat the grill to high (you can also cook the kebabs on a griddle pan or barbecue).

5 Thread the vegetables and tofu – I used 2 pieces of each type – onto the wooden kebab sticks.

6 Grill the kebabs for 10 minutes, turning them occasionally, until golden in places. Serve with wedges of lime for squeezing over and your favourite dipping sauce. Rice, quinoa or roti are good, too.

ON THE SIDE!

....

WHAT YOU NEED:

250g plain flour

½ teaspoon sea salt

½ teaspoon all-purpose
seasoning

1½ tablespoons mild
curry powder

50g vegan butter, melted

2 tablespoons sunflower oil

MY ROTI

I love roti! It's such an easy bread to make, no yeast, no kneading... I also love to add a bit of curry powder to the dough, just to give another level of flavour.

1 Put the flour, salt, all-purpose seasoning and curry powder into a mixing bowl and give it a mix.

2 Stir in the melted vegan butter and 125ml water, first with a fork and then your hands and shape into a ball of dough.

3 Tip the dough onto a lightly floured work surface and shape into a long rectangle. Slice the dough into 6 equal-size pieces and roll each one into a ball.

4 Take one of the pieces and roll it out into a thin round with a rolling pin.

5 Make a vertical cut down the middle of the round to the centre. Spread 1 teaspoon of the oil over the top with your hands, or use the back of a spoon.

6 Roll the dough up into an ice cream-cone shape. Fold over the top and push it into the centre of the cone, then do the same with the bottom.

7 Shape the dough into a ball again, then roll out into a round – it should be as flat as a 20p coin.

8 Heat a dry frying pan over a high heat. When the pan is hot, carefully put the roti into the pan. Cook for 1½–2 minutes on each side until it bubbles up and turns golden in places. Wrap in foil to keep warm and repeat with the rest of the dough until you have made six roti.

WHAT YOU NEED:

115g white cabbage, shredded

115g red cabbage, shredded

1 large carrot, coarsely grated

½ small red onion, thinly sliced

1 small red pepper, deseeded
and thinly sliced

125g vegan mayonnaise

Juice of ½ lemon

2 tablespoons chopped fresh
coriander (optional)

Salt & black pepper

CRUNCHY COLOURFUL COLESLAW

Packed with colourful, healthy vegetables, this crunchy coleslaw is a great side to vegan burgers, wraps and pizza.

1 Using a sharp knife, thinly slice the white and red cabbage, or you could coarsely grate it. Put the cabbage in a serving bowl.

2 Add the grated carrot, thinly sliced red onion and thinly sliced red pepper to the bowl.

3 Add the vegan mayo and lemon juice and stir until everything is mixed together nicely. Season with salt and pepper and scatter over the coriander, if using. It's now ready to serve or keep in the fridge for up to 2 days.

Serves 4
Takes 35 minutes

WHAT YOU NEED:

1 tablespoon sunflower oil

1 onion, chopped

3 garlic cloves, finely chopped

1 teaspoon dried thyme

½ teaspoon all-purpose seasoning

½ teaspoon ground allspice

300g brown basmati rice, rinsed

400g tin red kidney beans, not drained

400g tin coconut milk

1 Scotch bonnet chilli, left whole don't chop! (optional)

Salt & black pepper

RICE 'N' PEAS

This is a traditional Jamaican rice dish, flavoured with thyme and allspice, and my favourite Scotch bonnet chilli! The peas aren't peas at all, they're actually kidney beans.

1 Heat the oil in a saucepan over a medium heat. Add the onion and cook, stirring occasionally, for 5 minutes until softened. Add the garlic and thyme and cook for another 1 minute.

2 Stir in the rice, all-purpose seasoning, allspice and red kidney beans and the liquid from the can. Add the Scotch bonnet, if using, then pour in the coconut milk.

3 Pour in enough cold water to cover the rice by 1cm and bring to the boil. Turn the heat down to the lowest setting and cover the pan with a lid. Simmer gently for 20 minutes or until the rice is tender and the water and coconut milk have been absorbed.

4 Remove the Scotch bonnet and season with salt and pepper to taste. Spoon into a serving bowl – you can scatter over some fresh coriander leaves to add a bit of extra colour if you like.

DID YOU KNOW?
Rice is one of the most important food crops grown
throughout the world – feeding billions of people everyday.

DID YOU KNOW?
Peri-peri is a mix of herbs, spices and
seasonings – it's also called piri-piri.

Serves 4
Takes 1 hour, plus soaking

WHAT YOU NEED:

5 white baking potatoes, about 750g, skin left on and cut length-ways into thick wedges

1 teaspoon garlic powder

1 teaspoon peri-peri spice mix

2 tablespoons olive oil

Salt & black pepper

PERI-PERI WEDGES

If you love spices you'll love my potato wedges! But don't worry you can leave them out if you prefer – they still taste great! Serve as a side with vegan mayo or ketchup.

1 Put the potatoes in a large mixing bowl and pour over enough cold water to cover. Stir in ½ teaspoon salt. Leave to soak for 30 minutes. Swish the potatoes around with your hands, then drain and pat dry with kitchen paper. Soaking the potatoes first helps your wedges to crisp up when roasted.

2 Preheat the oven to 200°C/400°F/Gas 6.

3 Meanwhile, mix together the garlic powder, peri-peri spice mix and the olive oil in a large mixing bowl. Season with salt and pepper.

4 Add the potato wedges to the bowl and turn them with your hands to coat in the spice oil.

5 Tip the wedges onto a large baking tray and spread out evenly – you may need to use 2 trays. Roast for 45–50 minutes, carefully turning once, until golden brown. They're now ready to eat with your favourite dip!

WHAT YOU NEED:

1 uncooked beetroot, peeled
and coarsely grated

2 celery sticks, thinly sliced

1 small cucumber, quartered
lengthways, deseeded and cut
into small pieces

3 spring onions, thinly sliced

For the dressing:

Juice of ½ lemon

Juice of 1 lime

1 tablespoon olive oil

Salt & black pepper

ZINGY BEETROOT SALAD

A crunchy, colourful salad with a zingy citrus dressing. It's a good idea to wear rubber gloves when grating the beetroot, otherwise you'll get pink hands!

1 Put the coarsely grated beetroot, thinly sliced celery, chopped cucumber and thinly sliced spring onions in a serving bowl.

2 To make the dressing, using a fork or small balloon whisk, mix together the lemon and lime juice with the olive oil. Season with salt and pepper to taste. Now it's ready to serve!

DID YOU KNOW?
Beetroot is a root vegetable, like carrots, parsnips and yams, and because it grows underground, it absorbs nutrients from the soil.

YUMMY EVER AFTER!

WHAT YOU NEED:

1 small pineapple, skin and core removed and cut into small chunks

1 mango, peeled, stoned and cut into small chunks

3 handfuls of strawberries, halved if large

2 kiwis, peeled and cut into small chunks

2 handfuls of red seedless grapes, halved if large

1 green-skinned apple, quartered, cored and cut into small chunks

Juice of ½ lemon

TROPICAL FRUIT SALAD

I've chosen some of my favourite fruits here, but you can swap for your own. Papaya, lychees, dragon fruit, raspberries, blackberries and melon are all delicious, too.

1 Using a sharp knife, cut the green leaves off the pineapple and stand it upright on a chopping board. Carefully cut away the skin, slicing from top to bottom. Cut the pineapple into 1.5cm thick round slices and then cut each slice into quarters. Slice off the hard core in the middle and cut the fruit into bite-size chunks.

2 Slice the mango lengthways on either side of the large stone in the middle, cutting as close to the stone as possible. Make criss-cross diagonal cuts in each half taking care not to cut through the skin. Take one half in your hand and gently push out the fruit, slice off the cubes, then repeat with the second half.

3 To prepare the rest of the fruit. Halve the strawberries, if large. Peel the kiwis and cut into chunks. Halve the grapes, if large. Quarter the apple, remove the core, then cut into chunks.

4 Now the hard bit is done, put all your tasty fruits into a serving bowl. Squeeze the juice from the lemon all over the fruit and mix together gently and serve.

DID YOU KNOW?

Apples are one of the most popular fruits in the world and provide a great range of health benefits. The lemon juice will stop the apple turning brown after it has been sliced.

DID YOU KNOW?
Agar agar is made from seaweed
and is a vegan alternative to gelatine,
made from animal bones. It helps the jelly to set.

WHAT YOU NEED:

For the coconut jelly:

400g tin coconut milk

2 tablespoons maple syrup

½ teaspoon agar agar flakes

1 teaspoon vanilla extract

For the mango jelly:

250g tin mango purée

½ teaspoon agar agar flakes

1 tablespoon maple syrup

Coconut chips, to decorate
(optional)

MANGO & COCONUT JELLIES

These are so good – there's a layer of coconut jelly, topped with a second layer of mango jelly. A taste of sunshine!

1 To make the coconut jelly, put the coconut milk and 2 tablespoons maple syrup in a small pan. Using a small balloon whisk, whisk in ½ teaspoon agar agar flakes. Bring to the boil over a medium-low heat without stirring. When the mixture just starts to bubble, turn the heat to low and simmer for 10 minutes, stirring often, until thickened slightly.

2 Carefully strain the coconut mixture through a small sieve into four small glasses to make an even layer, then chill in the fridge for 2–4 hours until set.

3 To make the mango jelly, put the mango purée and 1 tablespoon maple syrup in a small pan. Using a small balloon whisk, whisk in ½ teaspoon agar agar flakes. Bring to the boil over a medium-low heat without stirring. When the mixture just starts to bubble, turn the heat to low and simmer for 5 minutes, stirring often, until thickened slightly. Leave to cool slightly.

4 Pour the mango mixture over the coconut jelly in the four small glasses. Put the glasses back in the fridge for another 1 hour to set. Decorate with coconut chips sprinkled over the top, if you like, just before serving.

WHAT YOU NEED:

For the crumble topping:

150g plain flour

85g vegan butter, cut into bite-size pieces, chilled

100g light soft brown sugar

25g porridge oats

For the fruit base:

8 purple plums, about 650g, halved, stoned and chopped

200g blackberries

½ teaspoon ground nutmeg

1 tablespoon demerara sugar, for sprinkling

PLUM & BLACKBERRY CRUMBLE

A favourite pudding for a cold day, feel free to swap the fruit for your own choice, or depending on what's in season. Great with dairy-free custard, ice cream or cream!

1 Preheat the oven to 180°C/350°F/Gas 4.

2 To make the crumble topping, put the flour in a mixing bowl with the vegan butter and rub with your fingertips to make a nice, coarse crumbly mixture. Stir in 75g of the light brown sugar and the oats. Chill the mixture in the fridge while you make the fruit base.

3 Cut the plums in half around the middle, take out the stones, then chop the fruit.

4 Put one of the plums and a handful of blackberries, the nutmeg and the rest of the light soft brown sugar into a blender and blend until smooth.

5 Pour the blended fruit mixture into a mixing bowl and stir in the rest of the plums and blackberries. Taste to make sure it's sweet enough and add a bit more sugar if the fruit is still too sour. Spoon the fruit mixture into four individual baking dishes or one large ovenproof dish.

6 Scatter the crumble on top of the fruit in an even layer and sprinkle over some demerara sugar. Bake for 45 minutes until nice and golden on top.

DID YOU KNOW?
Bananas are great for giving you a burst of energy – that's why athletes like to eat them.

WHAT YOU NEED:

4 ripe bananas, peeled and mashed

50g golden caster sugar

1 teaspoon vanilla extract

¼ teaspoon ground nutmeg

½ teaspoon ground cinnamon

A pinch of salt

4 tablespoons almond milk

125g plain flour

½ teaspoon baking powder

Coconut oil, for frying

BANANA FRITTERS

Everyone loves banana fritters – me included! And these ones comes with a touch of cinnamon. I like to serve them with coconut yogurt, lots of fruit and a drizzle of maple syrup.

1 Mash the bananas and brown sugar with a fork in a large mixing bowl.

2 Now stir in the vanilla, nutmeg, cinnamon and salt with a wooden spoon. Mix in the almond milk.

3 Gradually, mix in the flour and baking powder to make a thick batter. Leave to rest for 10 minutes.

3 Melt enough coconut oil to coat the bottom of a large frying pan over a medium heat.

4 Add a large spoonful (about 3 tablespoons) of the batter to the pan for each fritter – you should be able to cook about 3 at a time. Cook the fritters for 1½–2 minutes on each side, using a spatula to turn them. Continue until you have made 12 fritters – drain on kitchen paper and keep warm in a low oven.

5 Serve the fritters with coconut yogurt and your favourite fruit by the side and pour over maple syrup. And there you have Banana Fritters!

WHAT YOU NEED:

75g shelled pistachio nuts

75g whole blanched almonds

140g extra-virgin coconut oil

100g vegan plain chocolate,
broken into pieces

40g vegan cocoa powder or
cacao powder

4 tablespoons maple syrup

2 tablespoons plant-based milk

55g dried mango, cut
into small pieces

75g vegan marshmallows,
halved if large

75g Rich Tea biscuits,
broken into chunks

ROCKY ROAD

Packed with vegan marshmallows, biscuits, dried mango, nuts and dairy-free plain chocolate, this rocky road is the best!

1 Preheat the oven to 170°C/325°F/Gas 3. Line an 18cm square baking tin with baking paper.

2 Put the pistachios and almonds on a large baking tray and toast in the oven for 10–15 minutes, turning occasionally, until light golden brown. Remove from the oven and leave to cool.

3 Meanwhile, melt the coconut oil and plain chocolate in a small pan over a low heat. Beat in the cocoa powder, then leave to cool slightly.

4 Mix together the maple syrup and plant milk in a mixing bowl. Using a balloon whisk, slowly whisk in the melted chocolate mixture.

5 Roughly chop the roasted nuts, then mix them with the mango, marshmallows and biscuits in a large mixing bowl. Take out a handful of the mixture and save for later.

6 Add the chocolate mixture to the bowl of nuts, marshmallows and biscuits and mix together well, so all the pieces are coated. Spoon into the lined baking tin and level the top with the back of the spoon.

7 Sprinkle the reserved nut mixture over the top and press down lightly to help them stick. Chill for about 1 hour, or until firm. Cut into 12 pieces and enjoy!

WHAT YOU NEED:

225g vegan sweetmeal biscuits
(like Digestives), crushed

100g vegan butter, melted

½ teaspoon ground cinnamon

450g vegan cream cheese

2 teaspoons vanilla extract

175g coconut cream

80g icing sugar, sifted

Finely grated zest of
1 small unwaxed lemon

250g strawberries

Squeeze of lemon juice

1 nectarine, halved, stone
removed and sliced

STRAWBERRY COCONUT CHEESECAKE

This fruity cheesecake is sure to impress your friends and family. What's more, it's completely dairy-free!

1 Line the base of a 20cm round, loose-bottomed cake tin with baking paper.

2 Crush the biscuits with a rolling pin until they turn into fine crumbs. It's less messy if you put them in a small bag first!

3 Put the crushed biscuits into a mixing bowl and stir in the melted vegan butter and cinnamon until combined.

4 Spoon the biscuit mixture into the lined cake tin and spread out evenly, pressing it down with the back of a spoon to make an even base. Chill in the fridge for about 20 minutes to firm up while you make the topping.

5 Using an electric hand whisk, mix together the cream cheese, vanilla extract, coconut cream and 75g of the icing sugar in a large mixing bowl until light and creamy. Stir in the lemon zest.

6 When the base is firm, spoon the cream cheese mixture on top and spread out evenly. Place in the freezer for 2 hours or until firm.

7 To make the strawberry topping, using a blender, purée 175g of the strawberries with the rest of the icing sugar and a squeeze of lemon juice until smooth.

8 Take the cheesecake out of the freezer about 1 hour before serving, then carefully remove from the tin. Put the cheesecake on a serving plate and spoon the strawberry sauce on top, letting it drizzle down the sides. Decorate with the remaining strawberries and nectarine slices. Delicious!

DID YOU KNOW?
Flaxseeds are also called linseeds. This small seed can be ground up and makes a great alternative to eggs in vegan baking.

WHAT YOU NEED:

2 tablespoons ground flaxseeds

125g self-raising flour

70g ground almonds

50g cocoa powder

¼ teaspoon baking powder

¼ teaspoon salt

100g dried sour cherries, halved

125g vegan plain chocolate

80g vegan butter

250g golden caster sugar

5 tablespoons plant-based milk

1½ teaspoons vanilla extract

CHERRY BROWNIES

Super chocolatey with a fudgey middle – no one will believe these brownies are vegan! If you don't like cherries you can use raisins or dried mango instead.

1 Preheat the oven to 180°C/350°F/Gas 4. Grease and line the base of a 20cm square baking tin with baking paper.

2 Mix the ground flaxseeds with 6 tablespoons water and set aside for about 20 minutes until they form a jelly-like texture.

3 Meanwhile, put the flour, almonds, cocoa powder, baking powder and salt in a mixing bowl and stir until combined. Mix in the dried cherries.

4 Melt the plain chocolate with the butter in a small pan over a low heat. Pour into a separate mixing bowl and add the caster sugar.

5 Whisk together the melted chocolate mixture and caster sugar until the sugar dissolves. Stir in the plant milk, vanilla and soaked flaxseeds until combined.

6 Using a wooden spoon, stir the chocolate mixture into the flour mixture. Spoon into the prepared baking tin and level the top with a spatula. Bake for 35–45 minutes until cooked and firm to the touch – it should still be a bit squidgy in the middle.

7 Leave to cool in the tin, then turn out onto a wire rack, cut into 12 squares and dig in.

HELPFUL WEIGHTS & MEASURES

Millilitre (ml) = a volume/liquid measure

1 teaspoon (tsp) of liquid = 5ml

1 tablespoon (tbsp) of liquid = 15ml

1 litre (L or l) of liquid = 1000ml

Gram (g) = a weight/mass of food that isn't a liquid

1 gram (g) = ¼ teaspoon (tsp)

15 grams (g) = 1 rounded tablespoon (tbsp)

1 kilogram (k) = 1000g

COOKERY WORDS

BAKE: to cook food, such as cakes, pies and bread in an oven using dry heat. The outside of the food usually becomes golden brown.

ROAST: to cook food, such as vegetables, in an oven at a high temperature.

BOIL: to cook food in a saucepan of bubbling liquid, such as water or stock. When a liquid comes to the boil it bubbles and is very hot.

SIMMER: to cook food in liquid, such as stock or water, in a saucepan over a low heat so the liquid is just below boiling point. The liquid can bubble gently.

STEW: to cook food slowly in a simmering liquid, such as stock or a sauce, in a covered casserole or saucepan.

FRY: to cook food in a frying pan in a small amount of oil or fat over a direct heat.

DEEP FRY: to cook food submerged in hot oil in a deep saucepan or deep-fat fryer until crisp and golden.

SAUTÉ: to fry food quickly in a small amount of oil or fat over a direct high heat, usually in a sauté pan (straight-sided frying pan).

DRY FRY: to fry food in a frying pan without oil or fat.

STIR FRY: to fry food quickly over a high heat in a little hot oil or fat in a wok or frying pan.

DICE: to cut food into small cubes.

CHOP: to cut food into small pieces.

PEEL: to remove the rind or skin from a fruit or vegetable using your hands, a small knife or vegetable peeler.

GRATE: to rub food against a grater into shreds, fine slices or powder.

BLEND: to mix ingredients together using a food processor or blender into a liquid or smooth mixture.

KNEAD: to use your hands to massage or work ingredients together, such as bread dough until it is elastic and smooth.

GOODBYE FROM OMARI...

NOW YOU'RE A CHEF!

Remember to share your amazing pictures and don't forget to tag me on social media. The kitchen is now your science lab – try experimenting with your own recipes, dishes and flavour combinations.

Always try to stay humble, be yourself, work hard, and remember - your flaws make you unique.

Love, Omari

· ·

FACEBOOK
Omari McQueen

INSTAGRAM
@omarimcqueen

TWITTER
@OmariMcQueen

TikTok
@omarimcqueen

SNAPCHAT
omari_mcqueen

YOUTUBE
The Mari Maker Show

Stay safe! Please remember the golden rules of online life:
- Think about waiting until you're 13 to use social media.
- Keep your location and personal information private.
- Be smart – don't agree to meet face-to-face with an online friend, or send them photos of yourself, until you've spoken to an adult you trust.
- Report anything abusive or that makes you feel uncomfortable to a trusted adult.
- Remember your digital footprint – everything you post online is permanent.

· ·

INDEX